T0146526

RAINBOW SOUL FOOD

Heart Opening Poetry

A LITTLE SPACE BRENT TALBOT

BALBOA
PRESS

A DIVISION OF HAY HOUSE

Balboa Press books may be ordered through booksellers or by contacting:

Balboa Press
A Division of Hay House
1663 Liberty Drive
Bloomington, IN 47403
www.balboapress.com
1 (877) 407-4847

Because of the dynamic nature of the Internet, any web addresses or
links contained in this book may have changed since publication and
may no longer be valid. The views expressed in this work are solely those
of the author and do not necessarily reflect the views of the publisher,
and the publisher hereby disclaims any responsibility for them.

The author of this book does not dispense medical advice or prescribe the use
of any technique as a form of treatment for physical, emotional, or medical
problems without the advice of a physician, either directly or indirectly. The
intent of the author is only to offer information of a general nature to help
you in your quest for emotional and spiritual well-being. In the event you use
any of the information in this book for yourself, which is your constitutional
right, the author and the publisher assume no responsibility for your actions.

Any people depicted in stock imagery provided by Getty Images are
models, and such images are being used for illustrative purposes only.
Certain stock imagery © Getty Images.

Print information available on the last page.

ISBN: 978-1-9822-2616-9 (sc)
ISBN: 978-1-9822-2621-3 (e)

Balboa Press rev. date: 04/17/2019

Contents

About the Author

In 2011, I was living in Calgary, Ab and was propelled by a force bigger than me into the Occupy Global Movement, where people from around our planet moved into tents in front of their local government and asked the question "What about us?" The forgotten weirdo's who were to right brained to live in a left brained society and began collectively dreaming of a better future, by working on it now. The poetry that was birthed in this book was a result of letting go of the current capitalist paradigm and moving into a calmunist culture. A culture where we work symbiotically with Mother Earth and grow together as a global calmunity, while working on ourselves, in our calmunities. This book is God's words through I have been blessed to receive that the channels of yoga, nutrition, and meditation. I am just a conduit for God's Love and am mirroring your best self back to you. We are One! We are Love! And We are ALL Crazy! Your Truth shall set you FREE! My hope is that this work inspires you to follow your dreams and tune into your heart as you are worthy, worth it, and enough, You Are God! I Love You ALL and send my Blissings. It is my intention to donate 75% of the proceeds from this book to World Vision as we are a global village,

Namaste

a little space

Rainbow Soul Food

Rainbow soul food
This is me nude

Raw, buff, and real
See how it makes you feel

My blood, sweat, and tears, live in here
Eight years of birthing this baby, dear

Dear genuis you are loved by God
The eternal pranic breathing rod

The invisible umbilical cord supporting us all
Loving, smiling, embracing each and every fall

Homefree

I choose to live outside
not to run and hide

I choose to be alive
not to work from 9 to 5

I choose to challenge myself everyday
not just to exist in the same old way

I choose to create from within
not to consume from without

I choose to be a terra-wrist
not a terrorist

I choose to smoke pot
not to worry about getting caught

I choose to sing out loud
not to stare at a chem. trail cloud

I choose to live in the dirt
not to be told I should go to work

I choose to live in the here and now
not to be instructed that I don't know how

I choose to Love from the Heart
and from this place we will ALL receive
the choice for a brand new start...

A Stem Cell

I Am a Stem Cell
Directly from heaven, I fell

I Am the God Particle
Omniscientally intrinsically Magical

I am a blank cheque for healing
That alleviates the pain your feeling

I calmunicate and nurture through cellular regeneration
Stem Cell Therapy performs Miracles freeing us from inflammation

The Wizard of Oz
Elevating the Stem Cell cause

Health and fitness is the new currency
This is made possible by moving from me to we

I can't stop smiling
From ALL the Cosmic data we are compiling

It seems too good to be True
So sharing, facts, data, and stories it is up to me and you

About the How

Are you making time, taking time, or doing time
Do you see the harmonics of the Universe breathing in rhyme

Are you excited, challenged, and empowered from purpose
Or are you wallowing in the past surrounded by surplus

Are you listening to your Heart and following your dreams
Can you feel your pulse quicken, dancing naked on moonbeams

Are you able to quiet your mind through the practice of meditation
This is the ultimate treat you can give
yourself for healing manifestation

Are you tapped in, tuned in, and turned on
by this moment here and now
This is the way to tune into God's Love and
alleviate all concern about the how

Adaptation

I am a chameleon
sometimes a student
sometimes a teacher
but always a friend

I am alive
sometimes seeking "calm" unity
sometimes seeking "calm" unication
but always alert

I am changing
sometimes seeking solitude
sometimes deep in meditation
but always cheerful

I am blending
sometimes listening to the wind
sometimes panning for change
but always patient

I am receptive
sometimes breathing in lotus
sometimes sometimes contemplating a tree
but always present

I am Love sometimes
a Lover
sometimes a Love-e
but always LOVE

Allowing Others

How a re you experiencing biofeedback
Does it keep you focused and on track

Is it enlivening your senses and feelings
Have you the realization there is no ceiling

Are you open and expansive
Heart centered prepared to give

Tuning into the present moment
Breathing into the enlightenement

Being the change that you wish to see
Allowing others to let go and just be

Become the Seed

I am the dirt
I am the fertile soil
Implanted with ideas
If I am fluffy and maluable
I gift a new beginning
As the idea becomes the new growth
These thoughts that I'm thinking
These thoughts become worldly things
Created from nowhere arriving now here
I give ideas feet and arms
I am guided to do no harm
I am a stem cell for planetary healing
God provides the fruit
Mother births the veggies
And we become the seed

Being a Bridge

What better is there to be
than a bridge uniting a conscious society

Know in your Heart that we are ALL Unique
by recognizing the inspiration in the mystique

Allowing the patience for Truth to surface
realizing we ALL came here with Purpose

Creating spaces where everyone can be heard
remembering the passing down of oral tradition
through spoken word

Sticking to Our Integrity and Priorities
becoming humble to Mother Earth's seniority

Being the change that we wish to see
regenerating relationships moving from me to "WE"

What could we possibly do to heal this global dis-ease
we can bridge the conscious human gap,
back to the Trees

Breakdowns Lead To Breakthroughs

In a conscious state of awareness all breakdowns lead to breakthroughs
As people let go of old paradigms that aren't working and seek Truths

The Truth that lives inside every breakdown of conscious matter
For the Higher Self Energy that lies within, never shatters

The Truth pervades in every waking moment
If you can listen closely and hold back your comment

Everything in nature breaksdown and
breaksthrough as seasons change
Thisi is perfectly natural and extremely common
in nature, it is not labeled as strange

If I didn't have the down swings, I wouldn't be able to
recognize the perfection and bliss in this moment right now
Be-cause breakdowns always lead to breakthroughs
when you get quiet enough to listen to your how

Breathing Actuality

Every thankful moment maked me healthier
As I side effect I feel wealthier

The love emanating from my heart center
IS recharging energy, for all who enter

This love is boundless and free
It only involves tuniing into me

I am nature and her magically wonderous landscapes
Remembering my ancestry has evolved from apes

I am a manimal heart centered in purity
Felling into the foeld and brreathing actuality

Butt Pickin

I am a butt picker
Not a bum thief

I collect unfinished cigarette butts
discarded and strewn down city streets

I squeeze out the unused tobacco
and discard the filters into the bin

This is a form of "calm" unity service
As I live with a cleaning purpose

From Cadillac butts to tiny ones
The road are being cleaned for ALL to enjoy

Cleanliness keeps me at peace
When I am tidying my home of Victoria's streets

Calmunity

Living in the moment
Loving from the stomach

Experiencing the winds whisper
Listening everyday a little clearer

Feeling the bass's shiver
Dancing with plans to deliver

Being a deliver of the message
Baring witness to the transformation of the masses

Knowing the truths power
Illuminating the divine shower

Reaching inside for discovery
Enlightening as a result of recovery

Healing conscious "calm" unities
Remembering oneness "calm" unity.

Cause the Effect

Be-calm the cause
And be-love your effect

Class War

What is the perfect word I could say
to allow all of your fear and worry to fade away

Does this word exist
That could get you to cease and desist

From beating yourself up about your past
and instead realizing that life goes so fast

By grinding in your heels
and really listening to how you feel

BY actually paying attention to your own ass for a change
and recognizing that any difference in class is but a game

A game created by the monopolizers to keep us so busy
so we would never have time for contemplation or taking it easy

We ALL came from Gorgeous Mother
Earth and Beautiful Father sky
and we will ALL be returning from human
form in the blink of an eye

So Embrace ALL of your fellow Divine
Spiritual Beings and begin Dancing
For class war is ending and humanity is
realizing it is time for Romancing

Coherence of Love

Feed the thoughts
That feed your soul

This is the process
Of returning to whole

The quantum leap
Has no ground underneath

It is yours to keep
By letting go of the past

This moment here and now
Is the precious power

The generous present moment
Is where you receive the Divine shower

The showering of bliss filled conscious energy
Providing teaching for all those who are seeking

Realizing your power through synergy
Feeling the full coherence of love

Cosmic Magical Elf

I am auto poetic
Loving from the mystic

I am alive in the now
Living from the how

I am aware of metacognition
Living from pure manifestation

I am a heart open to possibilities
Connecting through sychronicities

I am God, becoming aware of myself
Living from my cosmic magical elf

Cosmic Mirrors

When I react I go directly into my head
and stab directly for the Heart
with the force to take down a dinosaur

With the intentional of killin the me
I C in U

The me I can't let go of
and don't wish to deal with

But energetically ALL I am doing
is bringing the me that I do not wish to see
repeatedly back to myself
in every environment of my choosing

I am ALWAYS attracting what I am
in each moment

So choosing to respond
allows me the necessary time
to take a few deep breaths

Slowly moving back into my Heart
to allow time for contemplation
to naturally incur

I always manage to find me piece
in the form of the nearest green space
and my journal

As soon as I sit down on the grass
the war on my head stops
and the birds become clear as a bell

I realize that which has transpired
can not be undone

But it offers many valuable lessons
for both parties engaged in the dialogue

When I react I blow up bridges
when I respond I build bridges

It is easier for me to Love the cosmic mirror
& ALL of the me's
I see in you

Creating Sacred Space

To bring the peace
you must first be at ease

You must stay in the flow
and watch carefully for the glow

You must stay in the now
and listen closely for the how

You must smile and be open
this creates the space to let hope in

You must laugh and be happy
and allow others to be yappy

You must hug and embrace
this is how we create sacred space

Curing Hobophobia

Sittin on the street
creates the place... we may meet

Stayin in the moment
creates the space... we may meet

Grinnin from ear to ear
creates the frequency... we may meet

Greetin from the Heart
creates the peace... we may meet

Listenin with revert alertness
creates the calm... we may meet

Engagin in conscious dialogue
creates the transparency... we may meet

Respondin with Lovin intention
creates the equanimity... we may meet

Huggin to complete conversation
creates the freedom... we may meet

So next time you go for a walk
remember "calm" unication is the key to
curing hobophobia...and we will meet

Dis-Grace Islet

We are not looking for donations
but rather a do-nation

We will decorate messages on our clothing
and hang them from the trees
for all to be hold...ing

We create beautiful nature art
for all those who wish to restart

Restart with compassion and caring
for all those who are naked and embraced in sharing

For all those seeking peace and "calm'unity
we feel you energetically as we surrender to unity

The unity and oneness that encompasses us all
It is time to gather on common ground by dis-gracing
Grace Islet, and not letting her fall

To fall from the grace of all the children who have played their
by sending the message that there are still those of us out here
that still care

Humans who are not here to fight, but rather sit naked
as we allow others to release their fears, by finally allowing
Grace Islet, to remain sacred

Discipline

Can you trust yourself
To be responsible for your health

Have you the vagina to say
I Love my body enough to pray

To pray for the ability to remember to play
And quit putting off life, for another day

Can you face your desires and say no
Have you created this meditative state, to go

Do you have the discipline to just stop
While you calmly allow the tantric cream to rise to the top

Doggie Style

I wish I had a tail to chase
I'd chase it around with my face

I wish I had someone to throw a ball for me
I'd be so phreakin happy, you would see

I wish I could go and jump in a lake
But this leash won't let me, for God's sake

I wish I could go run around outdoors
But we don't have time before the closing of the stores

I wish I could go for a walk by the ocean
Yet as I look at you, I am sensing no motion

I wish ALL my smiles and panting
Could excite you enough to keep you from wanting

I wish I could cuddle and lick you ALL day
But my need for peeing, pooping, and play, get in the way

All of this wishing and not doing, has made me very nappy
Alas, it is time to doggie dream, where I get to do ALL those things,
and just be happy

Dreaming

Dream is a state of consciousness
that can be experienced in the present moment
and the more you practice staying aware
the more dream like your current reality becomes.
Bliss consciousness is dream state present moment
awareness that flows through and as us.
As we become more aware that little voice
that keeps nattering in our ear,
evolves into a cheer leader that has become learned enough
to take time outs and just bare witness to the beauty of
Mother Earth and how she is constantly creating.
If you don't dream you are not taking enough
time for yourself and need to slow down.
Dreaming is extremely natural and happens when
you are relaxed and have a clear consciousness.
You can learn to put intention into your dreams and take charge
of your nightly movies and fly away every evening as I do.

Ecotherapy

Take a hike
Ride a bike

Get the Flock outside
Quit trying to hide

Go get some exerciser
Take time to recognize

Breathe in the fresh air
Remind yourself that you care

Stretch your body and imagination
While experiencing the ecotherapy play-station

Everything is You

Everything you are striving for
Is You
Everything worth arriving for
Is You
Everything you are seeking to find
Is You
Everything you witness being kind
Is You
Everything whole, perfect, and complete
Is You
Everything in cooperation, not here to compete
Is You
Everything your wildest dreams can conjure through imagination
Is You
Everything is possible, plausible, and pliable
in Our Holographic play-station
And It Is You

F.E.A.R.

F-uck E-verything A-nd R-un

F-alse E-xperiences A-ppearing R-eal

F-orgive E-verything A-nd R-ememeber or

F-eeling E-xcited A-nd R-eady

Fast

I have no time, no energy, and no money
Have you tried fasting honey

When we release our obsession with eating
No shopping, no foraging, no cooking, no prepping,
no cleaning, suddenly time is no longer fleeting

The body lacks energy when over consumption clogs our system
Slowing down and listening to your body, is true wisdom

All the crazy money spent on the purchasing
and transport to receive food to eat
Instead of sitting back nad relaxing into the
moment, realing you are the treat

When we fast we relax and let go as the distractions of life disappear
And the gift of our blissiplne begins to reappear

Feeling Misplaced

Patience is the virtue
Everything else is untrue

Simplicity is the way
Available every day

Compassion is the key
Give it to everything you see

Fear is let go
Now we watch you grow

This moment truly embraced
No longer feeling misplaced

Flying

Are you waiting
Or creating

Are you living
Or giving

Are you seeing
Or being

Are you connecting
Or ressurecting

Are you meing
Or freeing

Are you fleeing
Or flying

For the Parents

I have some ideas that I would like to share
With the two of you, because I care

The world is changing and growing in many wondrous ways
We are moving back to the future and re-embracing traditional days

I Love you both so much that I want you to know
I was blessed by your presence as you witnessed me grow

I realize I am not exactly the son you had dreamed, I would be
But I want you to know that I am safe with friends, in the trees

All you have done for me, I could never repay
And I'd like to Thank You, for allowing me to be happy, healthy, and
harmonious in every way

Forget it Just Love

Forget You Attachments
Forget You Expectations
Forget Me Attachments
Forget Me Expectations
Forget Egoistic Attachments
Forget Egoistic Expectations
Forget Attachments
Forget Expectations
Just Love...

Forgive it, Let's Play

Who would care if you didn't show up tomorrow
Would there be worry, fear, or people dealing with sorrow
Where would you be now that you are no longer here
Do you feel this transition would allow you to see clear
Is dealing with stressed out humans, so sad
Or is just thinking about it, making you mad
What could we do for ourselves this day
To alleviate societal pressure and not run away
Today, we can find the courage to express our choices
Empowering the masses to get off their asses and find their voices
Feel into your fear each and everyday
By saying ""Forgive it, Let's Play"

For the Kids

Wake up each morning with a smile on your face
excited from dreams of a happy filled place

Bring with you the freedom you found
as you begin adventuring and searching around

Follow your Heart as it fills you with joy
as you enjoy laughter with every girl and boy

Challenge yourself everyday to reach for the stars
as you find new ways to dance on mars

Fill your bellies with organic fruits and veggies
as your energy sky rockets you up the trees

Do your best to listen to what the angels say
as they flood your imagination with new ways of play

Create harmony in yourself
and you will be blessed with good health

Knowing that if things appeared to have gone wrong
that all that is necessary is to take a deep breath and sing a song.

Free Hugs

F-eeling of your Heart opening

R-eally becoming Aware of your space

E-mpowering your sacred Heart chakra

E-veryday embracing the moments

H-armonious Uniting of monkey's

U-nconditionally Enlightening each other

G-iving freely to the Cosmic reunion

S-erving Humanity and the Lovalution

Free

Feeling Really Empowered Everyday
This is how I choose to play

To live from the perspective of the awe filled child
Remembering to follow my intuition into the wild

Living free of the fear the death always seems to be drawing nearer
Sending Love to ourselves each time we are reflected in any mirror

Being open and joyess for the adventures today will surely be bringing
Feeling inspirations uplift while floating around the clouds singing

Just focus on being healthy and having FUN
Not stressing the details on how to get shit done

Free is truly my favourite place to be
It lives here in the garden, come and see

Freedom

I am the richest man I know
even though I have nothing to show

I like to sit on the street at your feet
wearing my rasta hat in hopes we may meet

I sit for a while maintaining my smile
knowing divine guidance has its own unique style

I bless everyone who walks by
even if I miss their eye

I bare witness to the evolution of our people
as they stop to chat instead of being sheeple

I am aware that this process is in motion
by the pure feelings of Love and Devotion

I am free to do whatever I choose
because my Heart knows that Love will never lose

From Above

Every moment is filled with grace
This is how I birther into space

I am present to the beauty unfodling
Knowing the future generations are ripe for molding

Molding into a consciously cognative growing hive mind
By experiencing the magic of calmunity practicing being kind

This is the rebirthing of our heart centered race
Allowing patience, compassion, and simplicity to elevate this place

Our Mother Earth and her beautiful bounty of love
This channel is but a frequency sent from above

Furry Friends

There is nothing like earning an animals trust
To be calm and patient is a must

Sunshine, water, and some organic goodness is all they need to survive
Being a conscientious animal partner is
the way to witness them thrive

Love, pets, cuddles, hugs, kisses, and attention
are always greatly appreciated
Because the more kindness and generosity you
show, the more it is reciprocated

Providing animals with a happy home and supportive environment
Will be more fulfilling than anything you'll get from the government

It is impossible to waste time being surrounded
by fury friendly creatures
As the truly are, our teachers

God is Our Government

The body is the mirror of the mind
To live healthy simply practice being kind

Find gratitude and compassion for lives unfoldment
Unconditional forgiveness, accaptance, and love is enlightenment

God has your back if you'll pay attention to the front
Realizing simplicity breeds needs as we let go of the want

Stay present and persistent and magic becomes ordinary
Remembering the blessing of God's grace is not so scary

Feeling intuitevly into each and every moment
Freedom is knowing that God, is our governement

God Why

God why am I so blessed to see
that we are nothing but Love
manifesting in this holographic reality

God why am I so blessed to hear
the whispers of Loving encouragement
your always whispering in my ear

God why am I so blessed to touch
all of these impermanent beings and
beauty you have created
that seem to mean so much

God why am I so blessed to taste
the wonderment and magic in the endless
supply of organic produce you make

God why am I do blessed to smell
all of the fragrances you've birthed
to remind me this is heaven
not hell

God why am I so blessed to be
aware of this message
you are delivering as me

God why I am so blessed to know
that everything is going perfectly
and conscious evolution
only knows how to grow

God why am I so blessed with this courage
because my child when you were birthed
everything you'd ever need
was included in your package

God I Love You
My child you have never been without my Love
and now
and forever

God why
My child "Why Not!"

God's Cosmic Awesomeness

I am not for sale
I am for share
It is the overly capitalist
That I do scare
Lying, cheating, stealing has been let go
It is Ethics, Morals, and Integrity that enlighten the show
Being the change, the strange, available to
rearrange through flexibility
Being right here, right now, patiently breathing
in lives miraculously magic serenity
Opening to each moment with calm awareness of bliss consciousness
Feeling with an open heart, ready to be of
service in God's cosmic awesomeness

God's Quantum Affluence

How can you want when you feel whole
This is the language of my soul

Knowledge is the language of the mind
When I'm whole, I only want to be kind

Experience is the language of my body
When I'm at peace, I don't feel like being naughty

My thoughts produce the creation of my reality
When I'm present, I upgrade my personality

My actions are a product of my thinking
So from now on its pure Love that I am drinking

When my heart and brain are in coherence
I am birthing from God's quantum affluence

God

Get Fermented
You can be Reinvented

Become Oxygenated
You can be Rejuvenated

Live Inspiration
You are Manifestation

Seek Truth
You are Rhyme

Be Love
You are Magic

Show up Authentically
You are God

Goodnight

I am pure energy
Flowing through cosmic synergy

When I pay attention
I recognize my part in cosmic manifestation

The energy flows to and through me
While halo's are illuminated for all to see

My energy is limitless and boundless
My dreams become manifest as I let go of thoughts of less

Abundant energy is my birthright
All I must do is pray to God, before I say goodnight

Happy Every Y'arrr

Arrr you ready for this one
because its about time to have some fun

Arrr you prepared for whats in store
because this year we will be satiated with having less
and giving more

Arrr you excited for things to come
because this capitalist system is coming undone

Arrr you stoked for things to be changing
because Mother Earth is always in the process
of rearranging

Arr you pumped to embrace the masses
because evolution is providing the opportunity
to teach their asses

Arrr you jazzed about whats in store
because each one of us has Love
knocking on our door

Arrr you elated for "Every Y'arr"
because of the realizing
that U are a shining "star"

So get phreakin excited about this Y'arrr
by letting go of last year
and realizing you have come so far

Homefree and Lovin it

Now and forever forward, I will be the person I came here to be.
I will prove the teachings of being Homefree

I will be my Creative Genius unleashed
to inspire those who have lost there peace

I will stretch imaginations and cosmic boundaries
as I perform completely freely with the gnomes and faeries

I will be the Being from Our Divinely Conscious Mind
as I continue practicing forgiveness and being kind

I will Love U for ALL Eternity
as if I birthed you and you are me.

How Can I Inspire You

How can I inspire you
To recognize that, we are 2

2 parts of a global whole
That reconnects ALL our soles

What could I possibly say
To allow you to remember
you are the way

The way of creative passion, truth, Love, and intention
That reignites the consciousness that fuels your invention

Where could I possibly go
To remind you of this holographic 3D tv show

The show that you are the executive producer of
When you live in the now and become the Love

Why do I feel it necessary to inspire the masses
Because they get very inspiring when they, get off their asses

Into the game we have ALL chosen to be here to play
As we learn to Trust, Empower, Enjoy, and just be, everyday

How'd I get so Hairy, Healthy, Happy, & Harmonious

How did I get so Hairy

And why do some, find me scary

I let go of things that no longer served me

And allowed for patience, sitting under a tree

I realized primping and cleaning myself

Was never truly conducive to good Health

Health now is my number one goal

As I relax into life and breathe from my soul

Health organically brings me to Happiness, I find

As I recognize Our Oneness and remember to be kind

Happiness is a Natural Choice

When you Listen Intuitively to your Inner voice

Then Harmony with the Universe, becomes your way

As you are guided to miracles each and everyday

Harmony with life is the most Orgasmic thing, I've found

Through ALL my Adventuring, Traveling, and Searching around

This is why I've grown out my hair

*For ALL to see it is about Health, Happiness,
and Harmony, that I care*

How

Love follows me wherever I go
This is all I truly know

I am blessed with magical life force energy
Created through a cosmic listening synergy

I am a goat who seeks hi altitudes
Who is elevated greatly by a playful attitude

I am the creator of this blissed out 3D holographic reality
For my heart has been opened to breath in serenity

To be present, in the moment, right here, right now
Is the space where spiritual manifestation comes to fruition and
teaches me how

Patience or Patients

Patience please
I'm sorry... I don't have the time
I have been programmed
for immediate gratification

All Good things come to those who wait
Again sorry... I really can't waste time waiting
I must hurry to go and wait somewhere else

Lets sit down and talk
Okay seriously... Now your starting to get
on my nerves and can't you hear my phone
its going bezeerk

How do you ever expect to improve
your health and happiness
Now you are ruining my life
and taking me away from the stress
that causes this dis-ease

Now you are sick and forced to slow down
You must address the health and happiness
you fear soooooo much

Just to understand family, "calm" unity, and
friendship are the cures for ALL dis-ease
and infinite patience produces
immediate results

I Am Dance

When do I feel the most phreakin FREE
When I am dancing the ASS off the feet under me

What propels me to this realm of body movement FLOW?
The energetic pulses contorting my monkey, as I gyrate and GLOW

Where am I lost likely to get FULL on dance tribal?
In Ganges, Saturday market, Centennial parks marimba revival

How do I get soooooooooo inspired to lose ALL self-control
By listening with reverent alertness and feeling from my SOUL

Why? You ask... am I dancing right NOW
Because in my Heart, I know I AM DANCE, somehow

I Am Peace

I live inside you in receptive silence
From this space we let go of violence

I enter you through sun and moonbeams
Activating your love vibration through conscious dreams

I am the 3D holographic movie you are directing
By the divine light of conscious awareness your erecting

I feel life through the senses of your being
It is through your beautiful eyes that I am seeing

I am the Cure

in this cosmic co-creative consciousness
so pure
I am the Mirror
reflecting back to you, your
magic dear
I am the Bliss
still emanating from your
1st kiss
I am the Bridge
bringing you back peacefully from
your voyage
I am the Tree
when you lean on me, I stand strong,
while flowing with
the breeze
I am the Flower
reminding you to stretch and drink lots of water
while basking in your
sunshine shower
I am the Seed
bringing with us every solution to
end greed
I am U and U and U and U and U and U and U and U and
ALL of U are me
I am the Seed, Flower, Tree, Bridge, Bliss, Mirror, and Cure
in this cosmic co-creative consciousness so pure...

I am U

U are annoying, frustrating, agitating,
and get on my nerves

When I am annoying, frustrating, agitating,
and forget how to serve

U are Beautiful, Genius, Radiant,
and completely Divine

When I am Beautiful, Genius, Radiant,
and Magically without time

We are boring, lazy, resistant,
and uninspired some days

But we are recognizing Our Co-creative abilities
to inspire, empower, uplift, and recreate in
regenerative ways

As we continue evolving and rewriting his-story
By Embracing the Divine Feminine and oxygenating her-story

I am U
U are me
Together we are rebuilding a regenerative society

I Am Worthy

I am here to be healthy
not to get wealthy

I love to be funny
not to chase money

I embrace relaxation
not the play station

I seek honest work
not to be a jerk

I am here for Mother Earth
not to find out what I'm worth

I LOVE DAD

Dad you have been gone for 24 yrs
but I can still hear you calling me "Sunshine"
ringing joyously through my ears

I feel you spirits presence everyday
as I remember how you made me
laugh in so many ways

I see the family characteristics evolving through me
and thank you dearly for ALL the things you've
helped me to be

I don't think you would have picked this path for me Dad
but I know in my Heart, you think I'm pretty rad

Now I understand much more clearly why you were considered
a black sheep
because deep down in my soul, I recognize you were very deep

I can't help grinning ear to ear, when I sit with your essence
as you allow me to listen to my Heart, adapt your beauty, and
gift my presence

I Love U Dad.
I know, "I Love U too Sunshine"

I've had better days

I'm havin a bad day
Everywhere I'm goin
I'm being pushed away

I'm havin a crappy day
It doesn't seem to matter which way I turn
I am manifesting crash and burn

I'm havin a shitty day
Things are completely unaligned
And so out of sync
I'm contemplating having a drink

Suddenly the Universe brings me a smile
As a child who is out of my sight line
Bounces by joyously laughing and
And allows me out of my mind

WOW!!! Tears are welling up in my eyes
As I soak up the unadulterated bliss
Of the miraculous child who's
Now long gong bye

WOW!!! More Tears!!!
The sun has just broken through the clouds
For the 1st time in a week
As the sun hits my face and
I grin cheek to cheek

WOW!!! I'm HUMAN!!!
And needed to experience that
In order to birth this

WOW!!! The power of a child
I may never know
Thank You God for delivering
These Beautifully Enlightened Divine Beings
To liven up this show

WOW!!! Transcribing these "bad days" sure can
Be a powerful tool
To move out of my mind and
Back into the Celestial Christ Conscious pool

WOW!!! I'm CRAZY and STOOPID
But it looks like its going to be a better day...

Illusion of Two

Being aware of thoughts bubbling up in your subconscious mind
Feeling into the Loving ones, while leaving the others behind

Letting go of habits that stifle you're unfolding
Breathing Love into our Heart, beginning gently remolding

Knowing you are the creator and new growth sprouts from within
Realizing thoughts become things as we co-create with our kin

Taking back responsibility for thoughts manifesting your story
Elevating your consciousness by embodying in the glory

The glorious wonderful being that is you
Mirroring back our raw beauty as the illusion of two

In Giving we Receive, to Conceive

I gave up my home
for my Heart
and moved in

I gave up being warm
to learn to illuminate
my fire within

I gave up eating what I wanted
for truly appreciating any of offerings
the Universe drops my way

I gave up bathing on a regular basis
to bask in Mother Earth's
Magical Essence

I gave up complaining
for being the change I wished to see
and began regenerative solutioneering

I gave up competition
to enjoy the co-creative Bliss
of calmunal cooperation

I gave up the Love of a Special Partner
to educate myself about relationships
and cultivate those things in myself
that I wished in another

I gave up preaching
by leading a life to inspire others
to follow their owns dreams
from experiential teaching

Into the Music

I can't, I can't, can't,
turn you into the music
I shouldn't, I shouldn't shouldn't,
turn you into the music
I won't, I won't, I won't
turn you into the music
Or Maybe I can
Maybe I should
Maybe I will
Turn you into the Music

Just be

Be open to new possibilities
Be aware of new abilities

Be available to new capabilities
Be conscious of new stability

Be alert of new opportunities
Be present to new resources

Be free for new experiences
Be ready to shed old paradigms

Be peaceful with yourself
and be peaceful with the world.

Keys to Evolution od a Conscious Species

1. F-irst

L-ove

Y-ourself (Pass judgement on no one or no-thing remembering
we are ALL dealing with limiting beliefs and be Compassionate
by the Transparency of Shining Truth from Within)
2. Release attachments to outcomes (Just be present and release ALL
past experiences with a positive attitude toward the Journey)
3. Have FAITH (F-ind A-nswers I-n T-he ...H-eart) in the process
4. Follow your Intuition (The Student Within)
5. Cultivate Patience (Prana Yama the Art of Breath)
6. Contemplate Personal growth (Sit Silently in Nature)
7. Challenge Yourself (Try Something New the TSN turning point)
8. Meditate (Sit quietly for 20 mins 3 times daily)
9. Create Community (Host Potlucks, Create
Garden space, Host jams and/or dances)
10. Repeat with a bigger smile each day as we become
more aware of Our true co-creative manifestation
Power as a Singular Organic Organism

Let Go

When U let go
U let grow
and then you will show
because you already know
the way to let go

Life is

Shapes/sizes

Quality/quantity

Truth/fiction

Peace/war

Friends/acquaintances

Inspiration/perspiration

Being/doing

Seeing/believing

Love/fear

Life is Right Here
Your Cosmic Mirror

Life Loves Us All

You and I are anomalies
We are as unique and different as the trees

We come from a race of one
Divided into many for a little fun

To see divinity in one and another
Is to recognize there is no other

We are cosmic mirrors of magical stories
Embracing strangers recreating lives glory

Open your heart to everyone
Your conscience evolution will be done

Share stories, space, and time
Be-cause life loves us all when we rhyme

Life

Life becomes a treat
When I realize, I am what,
and how, I eat

Life enlivens in song
When I recognize this 3-D reality
doesn't last very long

Life is "Now" and worth Living
When I focus on the gifts, I have
been gifted, for giving

Life is "Peace" in my Heart
When I remember this day
is a fresh start

Life is my gift to our Magical Sphere
When I go from nowhere
to "Now Here"

Like a Knife

I am confident in who I am
I let go of all the spam

Just because you can't see something it still does exist
This is the miracle that allows me to persist

Science is the language of mysticism
The latest gift humanity has been given

If you love someoene lead a happy life
This cuts through bullshit like a knife

Limitless Possibilities

My mind is my movie
The programming is super groovy

I dance and sing to my favorite song
As the pictures and affirmations flow along

Bineaural beats hemi-sync my brain
Letting go of stories of pain

Subliminally successing my life
Alleviating struggle and strife

Being open to limitless possibilities
Living quantum through sychronicities

Listen to Your Goat Heart

Here is to ALL you free huggers
You annoyingly happy, dirty little buggers

You get in the way while people are shopping
Plugging up the aisles, causing unnecessary stopping

Not even being aware of the traffic jam
And standing in front of the canned ham

If I had to guess, I'd say
More hugging occurs in produce, anyway

Continue hugging in these awkward places
Knowing their will always be a hug for you, at spaces

Listen to your Goat Heart
It's your huggiest part

Living in the Flowment

Sometimes I forget
I am a phreak of nature
And a gift to nurture

Sometimes I forget
I am a talking monkey
On an organic spaceship
When I allow myself to be
Sucked into the bullshit

Sometimes I forget
I am only as good as
The people surrounding me
So why not uplift the spirits
For all to see

Sometimes I forget
I am a feeling, caring, dancing entity
And now is the flowment for clarity

Living the Dream

How do I co-modify a message
that enlightens my passage

How do I charge people for information
that allows me to release the monetization of disinformation

How do I exchange a gift
for money that will soon be adrift

How do I expect people to pay
for this knowledge that has come my way

How do I attach monetary gain
to a dream from Our Universal brain

How do I tell the Truth and deliver
when I have expectations of getting my sliver

Truly I do not know how to embody a financial surplus
But Living the Dream allows me to live my purpose

Locating the Button... Restart

When will we finally let go of the ego
And return to a Heart centered, here we go

We WE WE are a unit, a team, a magical
spherical bubble, on a bubble, family
You see in space time travel, I peeked at the
end and it ALL works out happily

As every new beginning comes from some other beginnings end
For we are but miracles made of particles, friend

16 billion or so yearsish and cosmically
continuing, while remembering
We are soooooooooooooooooooo small and tiny, yet represent everything

With Love, compassion, and respect in our Heart
We will rebirth anew daily, locating the button... restart

Longevity Consciousness

Think outside... no box required
Think from your Heart... no mind required
Think from your core... no distractions required
Think from your being... no doing required

Remember from your youth... batteries included
Remember from your smile... good intentions included
Remember from your imagination... dreams included
Remember from your 1ˢᵗ kiss... passion included

Feel from your sole... there is no hole
Feel from your intuition... the student is within
Feel from your spirituality... this is a holographic reality
Feel from your quiet space... for this is truly your magical place

Love Button

What is your Love button

Where is the place
that Divine Light shines

When is the time that
Universal Consciousness
glows from within

Why is the emotions that take over
and perpetuate joy filled bliss

How is through the feelings
as Universal Attraction shifts paradigms

The way to your Love Button is through your smile
as it engages oxytocin, serotonin, and dopamine

The key is to surrender and live in the Flow
as you allow your Love Button Show, Grow, and Glow

Love the Skin Your in

Before I was blessed into this body
I never worried about if I would be a hottie

I was the infinitely expanding Universe
But for Now I have time traveled back in reverse

Into this talking monkey on an Organic Spaceship
Remembering the Cosmic Excitement of Tribal Friendship

Being brightly colored, open, accessible, Honest, and Sharing
Knowing each of us is doing the best we can, with what we have
and Truly Caring

Each of us being a Fantastically Unique
Brilliantly Talented Expression
of Universal Mind
Realizing this by sitting quietly with Our
Purpose, Letting go, and Listening
for the channel to find

The Channel or Frequency of your Passion
Where timelessness lives and we re-embrace Compassion

I gave up my home and television, to tune into Mother Earth
And have never again looked for the remote
or keys, to distract, from re-birth

My Rebirth as I awake everyday and say Thank You
And the more I Love the Skin I'm in the more channels I have
to tune in and turn into

Be-cause when U Truly Love the skin Ur in
You Recognize that Authentic Joy comes from Within

Loving Mother Earth

Every master
was once a disaster

Every mystic
was once a mistake

Unsure how to partake
without a rainbow cape

Every rainbow warrior
was once a lot scarier

But now much healthier
and hairier

Everyone feels at sometime alone
until our hearts open to every home

Realizing Adaptability
Practicing Flexibility
Loving Unconditionally
Sharing Truth
Growing Trust
Empowering Growth
CREATING SUPEREREOS
LOVING MOTHER EARTH
Becoming the embodiment of the living solution
Is how we let go all pollution

Magicolution

Magic is what we are
It can not be found in a car

Magic is what we know
It can not be found on a tv show

Magic is what we think
It can be found around the kitchen sink

Magic is what we do
It has been found by me and you

Magic is where we go
And Magicolution is experienced when your in the flow

Me & You

I've come here for ascension
Not to get mixed up in the monetary 3rd dimension

Money that is killing Our Mother Earth
It is TIME for humanity to consciously rebirth

Christ Consciousness embodying the sympathetic people
Allowing the rainbow crew to wake up the sheeple

It is TIME for Mother Gaia to be fully Loved and Listened too
As she evolves daily in peace and harmony, for me and you

Me, Myself, and I

Brent Gordon Talbot, a little space, space, was reborn May 21, 2012
When I quit trying to purchase myself off the shelf
I became free of old stories, alive, to love here and now
I became a student of listening to my body, and letting go of the how
Sprouts, krauts, ferments, wheat grass, local organic fruits and
veggies, while practicing yoga, creates unlimited energy
I now live in harmony with my meat suit as we thrive from synergy
My health, my energy, my lust for longevity consciousness
An understanding of the mind games that create them and us
WE WE WE WE WE
RRRRRRRRRRRRRRRRRR FAMILY
Me, Myself, and I ready to surrender, let go, and live happily

Meditation & Me

All of lives experience for me is meditation
the more I prescribed myself, the less medication

The gap or still place where are thoughts are all gone
as I relax and get tuned in, tapped in, and turned on

This mystical quietude co-creating my tapestry
as I willfully surrender next to this tree

Feeling umbilical connection like back in the womb
cosmically rebirthing back into my monkey home

Every time, I take the time to meditate
it brings me joy and releases any hate

Meditation has allowed me to be
A mystique in the market place
A fully instinctive creature in the woods
A public speaker, student, teacher, doer,
and poetic dancer, for ALL those who wish
to see, the benefits of meditation and me

Messages From Above

A loving being cares for all things
This is the song their heart sings'

Being in harmonic resonance feeling the flow
Letting go of stress and embracing your glow

Breating calmly into each moment
Seeing through the veil of government

Practing meditation through coherence
Embodying while experiencing the difference

Standing up for truth and love
Following ascended messages from above

Miracle

Don't just talk your shit
Walk your shit

Don't just complain about it
Do something about it

Don't find fault
Find responsibility

Don't listen to fear
Live with Love in your Ear

Don't ever give up
You Are A Miracle

Miracles Grow Where You Plant Them

Miracles grow where you plant them
Why is this not our planetary anthem

Together everyone achieves miracles
And we are but miracles made up of particles

Working in the dirt planting our miraculous seeds
Working on ourselves as we slowly pull weeds

Finding our peace and equanimity in the garden each day
Watering, chatting with, and caring for our babies, in every way

Being astoundingly dumbfounded by the magical beauty growing
Knowing in your heart those cosmic little flowers will be showing

Finally baring witness to the miracles that
have grown where you planted them
Singing, "Miracles grow where you plant
them" this is my personal anthem

Mom & Me

Mom why are you always in my thoughts
because I love U

Mom who was it you'd thought, I'd be
possibly a shepherd sitting quietly under a tree

Mom what did you think me super power would be
to Love Unconditionally and allow ALL to fell Free

Mom when do you think I will ever grow up
well Mom, I've spent the last 3 yrs filling my cup

Mom where is it you can always find me
by getting out of your head in to your Heart, taking
a deep breath, closing your eyes, and U will see me

Smiling, Laughing, and Giggling, throughout eternity
that is my gift and curse, for being the Mom of me

Mom

Since the 1ˢᵗ time ever I saw your face
I felt the Love in my Heart, as we made our 1ˢᵗ embrace

I felt the warmth of your glow
That allowed me to feel peace, as I rested to grow

I felt excited to explore this new place
While being cradled by my angel, who created me into this space

I felt nervous from all the bright lights
But your Love overwhelmed me as you held me so tight

In my minds eye, I can remember it like yesterday
Even though almost 44 years later, it seems, so far away

Even though we are no longer easily geographically connected
The Love I feel for you, in each moment, could never be disconnected

Now, as I bask in the Loving energy I am feeling
I want to apologize for kicking beef stew,
pre-birth, all over the ceiling

As I am giving birth to this poetry
Which could possibly be a tad easier, than the birth you gave me

I have tears of Joy clouding my vision and watering my beard
As I sit smiling, remembering, all the Loving intention, I heard

Mom, I could truly never have asked for anything more
And was truly blessed by what life had in store

This journey I have been on to find out
That my Mother's Love, I am never without

I LOVE U MOM!!!

Moment of Creation

Excuse me, how much for a piece of mind
Oh, I believe I can assist you with that find

It is not a piece of mind that you seek
But rather peace of mind authentically unique

No amount of money has the ability to make this purchase
But rather just simplifying and letting go of the surplus

Letting go of all of this 3D holographic sensory manifestation
Tuning into God, feeling into each moment of creation

Mud Mouth

What do you say to a brother
from another Mother

What do you say to a soul
That often times makes me feel whole

What do you say to a man
Who always makes me think, I can

What do you say to a friend
That's always standing with me, at the end

What do you say to a comrade
I apologize for making you mad

What do you day to your shaman
I'm going to miss you man

What do you say to your teacher
Without you I would have died, for sure

What do you say to a gypsy
Every time you cast a spell you will see me

What do you say to a yantric cartographer
Keep creating your magic and this will all soon be a blur

What do you say to your enlightened master
As long as we keep doing what we are doing
there will be no disaster

What do I say to the Brother I Trust with my life
Soon we will be reunited and continuing on our journey
Doing the best we can with what we got
Teaching sharing, caring, and "calm" unity.
I Love you Mud

My Farmacuticals

The Magical organic seed that cannot be humanly reproduced
The Magical sprout with its cosmic curiosity
The Magical delicate beginnings into anew weathered world
The Magic limbs and flowers that shoot out when we blink
The Magical ability to be strong and flexible whilst reaching up
The Magical ABUNDANCE of fruit and
veg that are birthed for sharing

My Refusal to Capitalize on Humanity

When I have a new job and
I'm scared if I'm going to make it
I look at others and start judging or
copying as I try to figure out this new shit

When I work collectively I realize we are only
as fast as our slowest link
So, I empower the people to uplift each other,
so our ship doesn't sink

Immediately, I search out and befriend those in power
So I can make the most of each and every hour

Or I listen closely for intuitive directions
As we learn trust through actions and realizing there is no deception

When I compete, I loose my competitive edge
Because its every person for themselves, as we traverse the ledge

When I cooperate, I experience the magic of abundance around
As we recognize our magnificence and joy is re-found

I refuse to capitalize on humanity you see
And I remain patient, persistent, and a little crazy
in the trees

My Ultimate Goal

My Ultimate Goal is to have No-thing...
no regrets, no rewards, no refuns
no unfulfilled fantasies, no dreams unexplored, no journeys untaken,
no reasons to smile, no need to do, no need to see
no unhugged members of humanity, no chance to
express passed up, no chance to share left undone

I came here with No-thing, but a smile
and most intentionally will depart the same way

Everything came from No-thing
And my Ultimate Goal of No-thing
Is in Cosmic Process all the while

Never Alone

None zip, zero, zilch
None of it is real
Everything is but a distraction
From the Truth of how we feel

Our holographic 3D reality
Is but a movie creating daily life
We are disconnected from source
This is why we experience struggle and strife

Your presence, your smile, your embrace are your gifts
God's Magical symmetry becoming alive
Be humble, be kind, be patient and breathe
We are here to work with Mother beautifying Our hive

Open your mind and allow time for silent reflection
Gift yourself to Our planetary home
By being at peace and harmony with your existence
My message is simply from the Heart, you are never alone

Now

To live in doubt
is to live from without

To live in fear
is to live from the rear

To live in the moment
is truly the only thing to covet

To live in the present
is by Loving through presence

To live from gratitude
is by realigning attitude

To live from clarity
is to Love from sincerity

To live from Love
is to soar with doves

To live in the Now
is truly the only way how

Occupy Our Ohm

Shoot, shoot, shoot, the messenger
For they have an ascended passenger

Live in fear rather than trying on some new change
Or are we worried we may stick out and seem strange

Embrace your Divine weirdness and Love each other
Is this not the least e can do for our Earthly Mother

You don't know what you don't know and that's okay
Just remember to go outside and reacquaint with play

Each day is a fresh beginning to reinvent our Magical Home
By realizing just how blessed we are to Occupy Our Ohm

Of Infinitey

I am God
I am of mystical beauty
I am Love
I am reverently silent
I am Peace
I am available for wonderment
I am Serenity
I am listening to magic
I am You
And we are a cosmic mirror of infinity

Outstitutionalized

Just let me be at peace i the trees
Laying grounded on Mother as she heals my dis-ease

Please just allow me to live outside
For I am to transparent to run and hide

Inside your walls I feel anxious, fearful, stressed out, upset, annoyed,
angry, and judgmental
All tings that make me hate, scared, tense,
rage, like fighting, like killing,
and then extremely suicidal

I have no fear of death and beyond
As I become more conscious of Our Harmonious Song

We are Divine Light Beings incarnated in a
3rd dimensional holographic meat suits
I can not be disconnected from Mother by
walls, buildings, or even boots

For my connection to living, being, and working organically in dirt
Is to heal this planetary cancer caused by competition,
capitalism, and monetary work

So I must be allowed to remain outdoors
with my "calm" unity in the park
As we teach each other organic trust and
sharing, while feeling safe in the dark

When I reside inside, I get in my head, and can't help but to cry
As my thoughts become infused by things needing to die

While being outside allows me the freedom to remain in my Heart
As I grow personally and await the global conscious evolution restart

You see never to be in debt is no life for me
But rather to grow into the world as it evolves, back, to be free

I have been outstitutionalized by listening to my intuitive choices
But that's okay you see as I exist Healthy, Happy,
and in Harmony with ALL the voices

Ownership vs. Responsibility

How could I ever assume "ownership over anything
When Mommy birthed me into this, I brought no-thing

In my 44yrs of attending Mother Natures glorious daily regeneration
I recognize that, birth and death, happen in
each moment on this play station

I have through many lives departing our organic spaceship
One commonality was they were always in
a hurry, instead of Loving the trip

This incessant desire for something to make us happy
Instead of realizing inspiration comes from
your soul and makes U yappy

All of my Loved ones wo hae traveled from this magical sphere
Are now at peace with the harmonic resonance playing their ear

Your energetic body keeps movin forward,
without the assistance of time
Where as your monkey meat suit will be left behind

How could I claim ownership over this cosmically conscious jewel
For when I transmute, I realize earth is an
Adventurously, Co-creative, Embracing school

P-eace O-ver T-hought

P is for peace– the relaxed state of awareness
the equanimity and balance found in the calmness

O is for over– the quiet creative state of creation
the freedom to share and be with any nation

T is for thought– the incessant chatter that comes from within
giving it the space or gap to grasp we are never without

For 32yrs I have been smoking pot
& I'm sick and tired about worrying about getting caught

I am a good person who is living to grow
and each time I share a doobie it continues to show

I Love "calm" versation and learning from people
as we put a pause in the matrix and quit being sheeple

I live to smile and glow from my heart
and every time I have a puff its an energetic restart

I tell the truth as my life is my laboratory
that smoking pot has made my life a more interestingly creative story

So each time I reach for my ziploc bag of medicinal herb
I naturally become more at ease and ready to serve...

Patience or Patients

Patience please
I'm sorry... I don't have the time
I have been programmed
for immediate gratification

All Good things come to those who wait
Again sorry... I really can't waste time waiting
I must hurry to go and wait somewhere else

Lets sit down and talk
Okay seriously... Now your starting to get
on my nerves and can't you hear my phone
its going bezerk

How do you ever expect to improve
your health and happiness
Now you are ruining my life
and taking me away from the stress
that causes this dis-ease

Now you are sick and forced to slow down
You must address the health and happiness
you fear soooooo much

Just to understand family, "calm" unity, and
friendship are the cures for ALL dis-ease
and infinite patience produces
immediate results

Peace

If I do this
I can have that
Then I'll be happy

OR

I can be happy
do good
and have peace

Planetary Restart

Energy can not be created or destroyed
You can not be created or destroyed

You can be consciously transmuting evolution
As we are in Cosmic transmission each revolution

The Realization that you are God
Not worrying about who thinks you are odd

Tuning into God's radio broadcasting through your Heart
Breathing into each and every moment right here right
now creating space for Mother's Planetary restart

Poppa Squat

Having a squat to Love and decorate
has allowed me a space to share and create

I sit quietly in my hobo home surrounded by red cedar trees
embracing Mother Earth's healing energy of ALL dis-ease

Healing the dis-ease of a competitive capitalistic past
simply by knowing in my Heart are one and this has passed

This time of the needless hoarding of Mother's natural resources
by going out and planting some "Fuckin Seeds"
and finding out what source really is

It is the planting of something so infinitesimally small
and then bearing witness to the gifts as they grow tall

The seed has everything in it required for the regenerative process
all it needs is water, sunshine, and an organic
environment fostering progress

Progress daily as the plants stretch for the sun
while the fruits of their presence enlighten some fun

Poppa Squat maybe how I will be remembered
but my story will be elevated by how I nurtured

Practice

Practice undiscriminating virtue
And people will see you

Practice silent receptiveness
And the world will undress

Practice reverence for Mother
And see there is no other

Practice kindness for all
And have yourself a ball

Practice being at peace
And live free of dis-ease

Purposeful We

My lives ultimate goal
Is to fall in love with each
and every soul

Knowing deep down inside of me
We are but cosmic mirror reflections,
for each other to see

By truly listening to one another
Speaking Truths about ways to
revitalize Our Mother

Sharing wisdom through spoken word
For All of those who wish to be heard

This is the time, NOW is when we begin relistening
As it is Our JOB, not to cease, until Mother is reglistening

Quantum Field

*I am no one
Now this is fun*

*I am no body
Feeling like a hottie*

*I am no thing
Time to sing*

*I am no where
Without a care*

*I am no time
Not even a rhyme*

Reach for the Pot

Each time I reach in my bag for the pot
I am sick and tired of worrying about getting caught

Because some morons made a medicinal herb illegal
Yet legalize alcohol which cripples people

For 32 yrs have I been blessed with peace and serenity
while smoking my medicine and releasing anxiety

I love sharing my medicine with everyone
especially chillin in the park enlightening some fun

My medicine allows me to relax and let go
as life slows down enough for me to become aware of the show

Why would anyone take a plant so sacred
and fill it with the intention of hatred

My medicine has been tainted with lies
by misinformation created by the ones wearing ties

I hold no one accountable for the insane error
but it is our responsibility to light up in public and release that terror

We potheads are a sharing, caring, creative collective
so next time you walk by a circle don't be so selective

Sit down with strangers and soon you will find
that we are ALL sharing this beautiful mind

For ALL you shaman locked up in jail
Know in your hearts that evolution doesn't fail

We will ALL be reunited and free U will see
as we continue to gather and grow organically

Educate your friends and families
so we can relax and help heal this dis-ease

Now in closing I'd like to leave you with this thought
For the next time you reach for the Pot

Remember to puff, puff, puff, pass
As the day approaches when we can tell the cops to "Kiss Our Ass!!!"

Recipe for Success of Thee

Eat Right
Sleep Night
Live Light
Recognize Might
Dream Sight
and Take Flight
Cause everything is Alright

Remember to Play

To all you tie dyed, happy, healthy, and
hairy rainbow warriors out there
Please continue to spread your joyess madness,
in the strreet, for all to share

You light up my life, my happiness, and my smile
You make me want to say hi, hang out, and chill, for awhile

You are athletic, acrobatic, flexible, beautiful,
unique, and oh so very interesting
Your intuition you follow whole heartedly, remaining
curiously excited for the moment manifesting

Your magical glow can be seen from galaxies, far far away
Each time you tune back into your heart and remember to play

Remembering Your Cosmicness

Yes life you are pretty trippy
Even to a spaced in hippy

Every breath a new adventure
Slowing it down, being the cure

Being aware of the gift that you are
Remembering your Cosmicness from your star

Feeling Loves intention pumping your Heart center
Allowing time to seek peace and serenity for a mentor

Just being patient with yourself and letting go
It is very okay to be wrong, it means your trying and how we grow

Salt Spring Island Hugs

Oh Salt Spring Island, how I love thee
For never have I witnessed and injoyed
a huggier phreakin calmunity

I sit in centennial park, Ganges, on the grass, off the pavement
To be visually entertained by these hugging embraces of amazement

The amazement of the overwhelming feeling of being home
And that shift in my Heart, that needs no longer to roam

Because the Trith I have been seeking is oozing out of this
magical Healing Place
As this Island continues to challenge me daily, as I recalibrate
and uplift the frequency of space

For 5 months I have called Salt Spring Island, the best gift I
have ever given myself
As I continue on my journey slacklining, playing frisbee, free
hugging, and birthing poetry to recognize
my Health is truly my wealth

Salt Spring Island, Huggiest Calmunity Eva
While we continue shining Unity Consciousness
no matter what the weather

Salt Spring Island

It is time to party and celebrate
as we continue to release any hate

It is time to dance and have fun
as we continue to do the work
that needs to be done

The bringing together of ALL the wayseer's
as rebirthing continues back into waybeer's

The harmonic resonance encapsulating our island, is electric
allowing people a chance to beathe and escape the hectic

The magic flows from the quartz crystal space
promoting laughter, smiling, and "calm" unity, all over this place

Salt Spring Island, Thank you for allowing me to see
just how fantastically fabulous people really can be

Self Realization

If you really wish to heal
We must first get real

Become truthful with speech
Being aware not to preach

Stretching out a hand to reach
Recognizing when it's time to teach

Bringing your magical self
Embracing our inner elf

Dancing with faeries in the sun
Embodying patience by having fun

Sharing Heavenly Experience

It ALL began with over a billion racers
My tiny sperm shell was going so fast
All I could see was tracers

I was racing for something instinctively I knew
As I realized quickly, I had to stay ahead of the goo

Not yet having awareness of space or time
I could feel intuitively this race was mine

Not knowing I had 9 months to rest and grow
I penetrated my new egg shaped home and
became conscious of this holographic reality show

I felt no fear in my magical new space
As life was supported and growing
All over this place

I never worried about what I would be, do, or own
But rather, I admired the glow of my new angelic home

Every moment something new and amazing was appearing
As the miracle of my life began it's rearing

All of the sudden I was evicted from my flotation tank
And greeted by what felt like a spank

Since that day my whole life I've been searching to find
That peace I feel with my Mom, so beautiful and Kind

Sometimes

Sometimes I feel interconnected
Fully mirror reflected

Realizing my mystical preparation
Has lead to magical manifestation

Breathing thoughts into things
Embodying cosmic wings

Feeling the world surrounding me
Shining brightly for all to see

Listening reverently, humbled by loving compassion
Focusing on co-creative healing, and enlightening passion

Some-times it all makes perfect sense
Some-times it all just makes

Soulversation

Creation spoke to me today
it said, when did they forget about play

I responded do you mean fun
they are to busy trying to get things done

Are you saying they've forgotten how to be kids
it seems to me they most certainly did

When did ALL it start
when they stopped listening to their Hearts

Bet the Heart is who they truly are
it's the only way to become their star

Thank You

Every day, I'd like to Thank You
For everything you are and do

If I can make one suggestion
when we slow down, release, let go,
and allow the flow of perfection

Allow the perfection of you to show, glow, and grow
by sitting peacefully in nature and baring witness to Mother's
Magic as everything shifts, moves, and organically grows

I know not, what will be written, upon sitting down
Then the pen starts moving, mostly on its own

Thank You for being a teacher, student, friend
And this I promise... It ALL works out in the end

The Eye Contact of Love

I don't believe in bad people
I do believe in bad her's and his stories
The divinity is always ready to shine through
Letting go of debilitating spelling, embracing what makes you tick
Fully feeling into each moment from a state of calm awareness
Breathing in the cosmically magical life force energy of God
Arriving in the physical form with the gift of giving in mind
Going around Ganges, smiling deeply into the eye contact of Love

The Heart Chakra Journey

What is this thing called life
is it about all the struggle and the strife

Is it about all the things we don't understand
like the concept of beginning and end

Like the concept of being scared of strangers
when we feel in our Heart there is no danger

When we flow with intuition guiding our way
the Heart Chakra will be enlightening everyday

The entire Heart Chakra journey is only 18 inches you know
when you traverse the super highway from your head
to your Heart and just glow

When you traverse to this magical place
your Heart Chakra can't help but explode
a smile across your face

Your Heart Chakra is a place I can always be found
because that is where "space" was created
and likes flying around

Because this is the space of Peace and Serenity
that exists in each moment for your Heart Chakra to be

The Illusion of Two

I like to raise my voice
Knowing it is a powerful choice

I like to run around
Knowing that joy and fun are what I've found

I like to jump up and down
Knowing that to some I may appear as a clown

I like tie dye and rainbows
Knowing color lights up my soul, so it glows

I Love opening my Heart to another
Knowing we are all sisters and brothers,
sharing Our Magical Mother

I Love You
And the Illusion we are two

The Imaginary Power of Monetary Poverty

Every dollar we spend is the same as casting a vote
Which becomes next to impossible when attempting to stay afloat

The money we spend to gather survival resources
Is cut down drastically by Our lack of possible sources

Sources to purchasing Organic Healthy Meals
Will not fit into the searching for deals

Poverty Consciousness is perpetuated by the growing
As the Wealth Gap expands and Information continues showing

Showing the Universal Wealth "WE ALL HAVE TO SHARE"
As we Remember we are One and there is Abundance to spare

The Abundance that is found in Unity Consciousness
As Evolution continues forward and repairs progress

Progress back to this place in Our Heart
Which is available in each moment, for a Conscious Re-start

The Imaginary Power of Monetary Poverty
Does not exist, for ALL those who choose, to just Be

The Loft

The time traveling ever evolving art gallery
Where consciousness grows daily for ALL to see

The place to go to meet new friends and old
While admiring the stunning art as it unfolds

On crystal islands it truly is a gem glowing
From a place within ALL of us the Divine Light is showing

Chris continues to bring together the masses
To "calm" verse, hug, dance, or just shake their asses

A place where even the lost boys are found
Keeping busy moving and creating stuff around

A home for ALL time travelers to go
To be enlightened by the kindness yo

A cosmic adventure for ALL to enjoy
By sharing ideas and embracing the Joy

So whenever your looking for the best place to chill
Come to the Loft and experience and Energetic refill

The Magic Formula

Be present
Knowing you have been pre-sent

Maintain an elevated state
By putting love, pecae, and compassion, on your plate

See everything as an opportunity to learn and grow
Letting go of mental baggage in tow

Having no attachments or expectations to the manifestation
Working honestly. while playing in ourcommunal play station

The Magic of Rainbow

Do you like rainbows?
I sure do

Let's make my favorite
We put all the colors in a stew

The most phantasmagorical creation
Adding color after color the rainbow grew and grew and grew
Infinite colors gleaming the light of Love
Feeling lighter glowing intrinsically I flew, I flew I flew

Yes, I delight in the Magic of Rainbow
As it has brought me to this moment right here
and right now, bowing down to you

The Perfect Stranger

Down to the beach on Dallas road did we go
Ocian, Josh, and I, as we were in the flow

We climbed down the stairs to the beach
having no idea who are travels could reach

We cuddled up to some big logs
as we relaxed and began to dialogue

We had only been sitting for about 5 minutes
when we were approached by a stranger, who asked to join us

After exchanging names we had a new friend, named Peter
who offered Guinness beer, for us to share

He told us of his day wandering the shore line
and asked if he could share his poetry, at this time

From his Heart he began sharing his poem
which created the feeling of connection, as if we'd already known him

He continued by telling us about his family
which really assisted us in understanding his poetry

We sat together sharing, crying, and laughing for about an hour
when Peter announced his departure from our intimate pow wow

We learned many lessons from Peter, that day
As the perfect stranger, to complete the perfect day, went on his way

The Rainbow-less Rainbow

Today, I was struck by an astonishing spectacle in the sky
As I gazed upon a rainless rainbow through my eye

It was not the usual arcing shape
But ran straight up and down the landscape

The vertical rainbow emanated white light from its core
That touched my soul, opened my heart, and yelled for more

I felt filled with the divine rainbow light of intention
This allowed pure bliss to permeate each of
my cells with cosmic manifestation

Do not expect things to be a certain way
Accept life's lessons and choose to learn everyday

The vertical rainbow less rainbow taught me that day
That life's magical unfolding will always lighten the way

The Rest

My Heart lives in the forest
My soul in the sky

My body remains here and now
For the rest of now and here

The Secret

The Secret...
is to embrace each moment with a meditative
state of reverent alertness

The Secret...
is to enjoy every chance meeting as if it had been
guided by the Divine Light of Consciousness

The Secret...
is to expect fabulous miracles, while having no
attachment as to when they show up

The Secret...
Is to experience ALL of Mother Earth's treasures,
by nomadic-ally living this incarnation

The Secret...
Is there is NO secrets, you can only ever work on
yourself and you never attract what you want, but
rather what U are

The Union

A time for the people to gather
to dialogue on something other than weather

A frequency for us ALL to tap into
By letting go of what really isn't you

A paradigm of pleasure
While embracing your soulstar

A space that's created for ALL to meet
Even panners, buskers, bums, and hobo's
will be off the street

A journey into Our cosmic mirrors of Consciousness
By having a puff and holding your breath

Ascending Unconditional confidence in Our souls sista's and brotha's
As the blunts keep coming, one after another

Arriving back with a permagrin
And then reciting a story, that comes from within

Giving the people a place to go and share
Where we don't have to breathe in unconscious air

Thursday evening at 8:30 every week
We have a Union Meeting, for all those, who seek

The Way Out

Hired.
Tired.
Fired.
Inspired.
Retired...

The Wayseers

For ALL those who have chosen to serve humanity
you may not be noticed by a sick society

But know deep down in your core,
that you are doing the work
For a cancer ridden planet coming into the light,
from the dark

Your every smile is being warmly received
as we continue re-birthing and healing dis-ease

Your Presence and Passion constantly growing from within
as we alleviate consumerism and living from without

Know in your Soul that we ALL came from One
and Conscious Expansion is no-thing but Fun

Free the constant traffic of your mind
by breathing deeply into your Heart and practicing
being Kind

For ALL you Wayseers I Know, Love, and Serve
recognize this message is coming from Mother Earth...

They

Well they say
Who are they anyway?

They are those who avoid thinking for themselves
Those who would run from the fairies and the elves

Those who are tuning out there inner child
By staying disconnected from the wild

Forgetting the magic fairy tale of life and just being
By breathing into the moment and reconnecting to loving

They can and will start telling the true story
For all of us, they, and those, who choose believe in the glory

Thoughts With Wings

Thoughts become things
So think thoughts with wings

Your attitude
Determines your altitude

Your vision
Fuels your mission

Your purpose
To be of service

Your gift
To uplift

Your destiny
To Be Free

Time Traveling Space

I am not a lazy bum
but rather from the future,
I have come

To alleviate all your worry and fear
that something dastardly wrong is going on here

The Truth is that everything is exactly perfect right now
as Conscious Universal Expansion continues anyhow

The imperfection you are experiencing in your reality
can simply be released through deep breathing under the nearest tree

Bring you focus back to the present moment through meditative peace
as we continue our growth process of healing dis-ease

I am time traveling space this time around
in your happy place,
I can always be found

U Did It

Time costs money
holy fuck do I find that funny

Time doesn't even exist
for it is only ever now, unless you resist

Resit the programming to be human doings
by really feeling into each moment of awareness,
from a calm state of just being

Just being the miraculous talking monkey, you came here to be
by stepping out of your comfort zone and allowing everyone to see

What an Amazingly Courageously Gorgeous talking monkey you are
as we transcend duality by cosmically mirroring back our star

The star that you are and have always been
until someone told me "Time costs money" and I got mean

I lied, cheated, and stole every chance I got
thinking somehow that I'd never get caught

Now realizing through living this incredible
journey of learning by experience
all that truly matters is what you are doing
when no one else is looking
for you are the judge of your lives circumstance

I DID IT ALL to me
to see if they'd still LOVE me

Until I recognized that LOVING me was my Occupation
so I brought myself to Salt Spring Island,
the Magical work/play-station

Thank you for ALL being in this cosmically conscious place
and allowing me to LOVE my way into this space

You are A-BUN-DANCE

Abundance comes from within.
You were the creator of the good and bad things they happened to you.

It was ALL for your learning and betterment. There is no bad.
Money is part of history. Not the future.

We live in harmony by living off and with the land.
We work together in our "calm" unities and welcome
travelers to teach the stories of other lands.

We trust each other and ourselves to do the right thing, because we
finally quit talking and started listening. Competition is no longer
the norm, but instead we have returned back to the future where
cooperation is the key to a new era of THRIVAL over survival,
friendship over money, relationships over egos, and ethics over profits

U R the Gift

Inspiration
the spirit within

Intuition
the student within

Insecurity
the security within

Intent
the intention within

Inmate
the friend within

Instill
the still within

Ingenious
the genius within

Indoctrinate
the programming within

Institutionalized
the walls within

Incognito
the chameleon within

In-congruent
the balance within

Incomplete
the completion within

In closing
I would like to incourage you
to investigate the idea that
everything came included with the package.

Unconditionally

Freedom lives within side of you
It is the space of nonattachment
Freedom knows no boundaries
It lives in the stillness of quietude
Freedom stretches from your soul
It enlivens the holographic 3D reality
Freedom is listening to pain
It teaches while encouraging growth
Freedom is knowing God
God Loves Unconditionally

Unconscious Fear

The unknown has never let me down
The known keeps me acting like a clown

The mystery of the quantum field
Only needs us to show up and yeild

We are riding on the backs of giants
Now when we work together like ants

Whispering sweet encouragement in your giants ear
This is the process to let go of unconscious fear

Us Up Whole

Move through life slowly and life will move slowly through you
Be mindful of judgments and love wholeheartedly what you do

Consciously breathing in the free gift of pranic healing
Not focusing on thoughts, but instead being aware of how your feeling

The gift of a new day to try on something out of the comfort zone
Having the knowingness that with God, you
can never and have never been alone

My benevolent imaginary friend that gives life to my soul
Being one with Our Universal sisters and brothers,
as enlightenment fills us up whole

What can I do

When I say what I mean and mean what I say
I experience enlightened time travel in every way

When I smile for no reason
I am reminded there is beauty in every season

When I arrive already grateful
I am often times blessed by a plate full

When I show up with magical stories to share
I bear witness as we illuminate and lighten the air

When I lead by example and do right action
I am surrounded by consciousness and participation

What I Know

Education is true gold
It elevates above growing old

Interpersonal relationships are truly the key
As co-creation permeates throughout society

Sharing is a must
It is a process of building trust

Having a sense of humour about yourself
Will keep you in good health

Meditating on a daily basis
Creates a true oasis

Hugging opens the heart
What a great place to start

Blessing everything into your temple
Remembering the less, is more than ample

What I know is that you are a mirror of me
When I shine brightest, I empower all who see

What's in Store

When I don't resist I'm in grace
While I do persist in space

I am blessed just by being
Now with God's eyes I am seeing

Seeing the blessing in every event
Recognizing and realizing its been heaven sent

To teach, to guide, to liberate, into freedom
Knowing your are the messenger in God's kingdom

Your heart and brain coherence unlocking the door
For bliss consciousness to unveil what's in store

When I remember

It is always darkest before the dawn
Storms are always followed by calm

Consumption is the road to hell
Creation is the frequency of heaven

Boredom is an evolutionary tool
Inspiration is an oxygenated pool

Freedom is the only way
Treedom is here to stay

Smoking weed is my right
God's seed is out of sight

Laughter is real medicine
True happiness comes from within

Imagination is the key
For this "I'm" "agin" "nation" to be free

It doesn't matter where you are
When you stretch it out you will be a star

Open your spiritual heart center everyday
And listen closely to what the angels say

As you listen with your heart
You'll be shown the way and a place to start

You are God

Unconditionally love yourself
You are worthy

Unconditionally forgive yourself
You are perfect, whole, and complete

Unconditionally accept yourself
You are enough

Unconditionally you are worthy, perfect,
whole, complete, and enought
You are God

Your First Kiss

The Truth is a stubborn thing
For with it you must sing

Sing your dreams into beautiful humanity
Allowing them to let go of scarcity

Spelling spells of beauty and grace
Spraying magic all over this place

Living from the pure intention of God's Love
Knowing its time to let soar the peace dove

Everything emanates from nothing but frequency
The energy slows to particle form, for us to see

The infinite source of endless joy, love, and bliss
Remembering the feeling of your first kiss

Imagine...

Imagine...
You are a Divine Spiritual Being
having a human experience

Imagine...
You are blessed with everything
required for your journey

Imagine...
You have the ability to tap into
the Universal mind of Consciousness

Imagine...
You are growing and changing everyday
for the betterment of ALL human kind

Imagine...
You are reaching out to strangers
with Unconditional Loving Intention

Imagine...
You are guided instinctively to listen
to your Heart and live your Truth

Imagine...
You are Energetically Creating
everything that you Experience

Imagine…
You are God

Imagine…
You're AWAKE

The Truth

We are the People
We are the ones who have chosen to be here
We are the ones "Being the Change"
We are the ones facilitating the Great Shift

The Secret is...No Secrets

Transparency is the only road to Enlightenment

Our common realizations as Conscious Beings
We are Love
We are One
We are ALL CRAZY
and Your Truth shall You Free

Printed in the United States
By Bookmasters